BEHIND THE GREAT WALL OF CHINA

BEHIND THE GREAT WALL OF CHINA

Photographs from 1870 to the Present

Edited by

CORNELL CAPA

With an Introduction by

WESTON J. NAEF

EXHIBITION CIRCULATED UNDER THE AUSPICES OF THE
INTERNATIONAL FUND FOR CONCERNED PHOTOGRAPHY

Designed by Robert Goff
Type set by Finn Typographic Service, Inc.
Printed by The Meriden Gravure Company
Bound by A. Horowitz & Son

Library of Congress Catalog Card Number: 72-81646

CONTENTS

FOREWORD *Thomas Hoving*

ACKNOWLEDGMENTS *Cornell Capa*

INTRODUCTION *Weston J. Naef*

PHOTOGRAPHS AND STATEMENTS

    I *John Thomson*

    II *Edgar Snow*

    III *Nym Wales (Helen Foster Snow)*

    IV *Robert Capa*

    V *Henri Cartier-Bresson*

    VI *Marc Riboud*

    VII *René Burri*

FOREWORD

Behind the Great Wall, the fascinating exhibition of photographs of China shown at the Metropolitan Museum at the time of President Nixon's visit to Peking, drew a record number of visitors, eager for glimpses of the vast land and its people so long hidden from American eyes. They peered at snapshots taken by Edgar Snow and Nym Wales of the leaders of the already legendary Long March; they studied the documents of the professional photographers Burri, Capa, Cartier-Bresson, and Riboud, captivated equally by the absorbing content and superb form. The show, alas, could stay on our walls for only a brief time, but now we are pleased and proud to present it again—metamorphosed into a more permanent form—as a book.

The Museum is most grateful for the generosity of The JDR 3d Fund, which made the exhibition possible. Thanks are also given to The Helena Rubinstein Foundation, which contributed funds, and the International Fund for Concerned Photography, which contributed color enlargements and the services of its personnel. In addition, I would like to indicate here the Museum's thanks to Cornell Capa, guest director of the exhibition, as well as to members of the Museum staff who were directly concerned with the exhibition: Karl Katz, Chairman for Exhibitions and Loans, who along with Mr. Capa conceived the idea, John McKendry, Curator of Prints and Photographs, who made available the staff and facilities of his department, and Weston Naef, of that department, who assisted Mr. Capa in organizing the exhibition.

Thomas Hoving, Director

ACKNOWLEDGMENTS

Ever since the time of Marco Polo, Westerners have learned about China from other Westerners—travelers who brought back stories, descriptions, paintings, and more recently, photographs of the giant land that seems so far away. *Behind the Great Wall*, first the exhibition and now this book, was conceived of as a collection of impressions, photographic and verbal, by a small group of perceptive visitors to China.

When President Nixon announced his plan to visit China, my mind turned back to the period when my brother, the late Robert Capa, went there in 1938. How eagerly we awaited the arrival of the China Clipper—Pan Am's famous Orient-U.S. weekly flight—carrying his latest photographs and tales of adventure. In China, Bob met the journalist Edgar Snow and his wife of that time, Nym Wales, and traveled through the land with the American military observer Evans Fordyce Carlson. I became familiar with that exciting period of China's history through their work.

During the past twenty years, the European photographers Henri Cartier-Bresson, Marc Riboud, and René Burri were able to make repeated journeys to China, and through my association with Magnum, the international cooperative of photojournalists, I became familiar with their work as well.

Joint investigation with Karl Katz, Chairman of Special Exhibitions of the Metropolitan Museum, and Weston Naef, Assistant Curator of the Department of Prints and Photographs, led to rediscovering the outstanding Chinese material of John Thomson (1870). From London, we obtained two unique albums, compiled by Charles I. Lucas (1878) and his son C. E. Lucas (1912), of early Chinese photographs.

The sources of other photographs and texts will be discovered at appropriate places in the book. Here, I give special thanks to the photographers who furnished original statements for our book: Nym Wales, Henri Cartier-Bresson, Marc Riboud, and René Burri; to our editorial associates on the project: Margot Feely, Cheryl Douglas, Yvonne Kalmus; and to Magnum Photos., Inc., for its assistance in expediting the collection of the photographs of Henri Cartier-Bresson, Marc Riboud, René Burri, and Robert Capa.

I extend apologies to a number of colleagues, unrepresented here, who have also brought back outstanding photographic work from China. Limitations of space and budget, as well as a necessarily narrow focus, led to the present selection.

It is our hope that there will be other exhibitions showing work of a new generation of perceptive visitors to China. Through them, we can expect to gain a deeper understanding of a land that even now, through the shrinkage of the globe effected by telstar and photography, seems less distant than it did yesterday.

Cornell Capa

PHOTOGRAPHY and travel have been associated since the earliest moments of the medium in the 1840s. It is only by keeping this fact in mind that words about China and the history of photography make any sense at all, for the Chinese produced no pioneers in the medium nor did they contribute to the advancement of its technology. On the other hand the Orient possessed a magnetism for Westerners that created a wide market for any kind of picture that would make that far-off land seem less remote. Indeed, any print collection of size contains many sheets of engravings and lithographs of China, attesting to the assertion that there was a large demand for such images.

The interior of China was closed to most visitors from the West until about 1857. Had this not been the case, it is likely that our photographic history of the country would begin before it does. Had the country been fully open to travelers in the forties and early fifties, some enterprising daguerreotypist probably would have visited there, and we would now have a body of valuable images of monuments, doubtless including the Summer Palace before it was bombarded during the Anglo-French aggressions of 1857. Had there been a strong colony of British in China in the same period, we would probably have calotypes similar to those made in India by British colonials, who, with an excess of leisure time, took up photography at an early date.[1]

The first photographers of record to have visited China are mentioned in the report of Commodore Matthew C. Perry's expedition to the Far East in 1852–54, wherein are mentioned the daguerreotypists E. Brown, Jr., and one Draper. Included in this report, *Narrative of the Expedition to the China Seas and Japan*, edited by Francis I. Hawks and published in 1856, are lithographs after that group of daguerreotypes (now lost) taken along the coast of China. The earliest photographs from China to have survived in numbers are commercially produced cartes de visite.[2] These images, which first appear in the last quarter of the fifties, are albumen prints measuring about 2½ by 3½ inches, mounted on cards, generally showing the native types, their occupations, and to a lesser extent, views of cities and picturesque land-

Photographers unknown. Cartes de visite, about 1857. Private collection, New York.

Felice Beato. Rear of the North Fort, Near Peking, 1860. Nilva collection, New York.

scapes. Precursors of post cards, they were produced primarily for visitors to take back home. Most were taken by uninspired local photographers. Other photographs were made to fill the needs of people who wanted to travel but could not. These were generally the work of photographers from the West, whose negatives could be duplicated in large numbers at home.

Among the earliest such traveling photographers whose name has come down to us was Felice Beato. He had learned the albumen-on-glass technique from Roger Fenton with whom he had worked in the mid-fifties photographing the Crimean War.[3] Beato, even more than Fenton, was at home in the midst of a fracas, and has today more of a reputation for capturing newsworthy moments of violence than for his numerous architectural views. In Peking during the Franco-British Wars of 1857–60, Beato photographed the carnage at the battle of Fort Taku, where many Chinese were slaughtered, and at the Summer Palace shortly after it was burned by the Europeans. It does not appear that Beato traveled extensively in China, since his extant photographs are from a relatively circumscribed area around Peking. It is not surprising that he traveled little, for his photographic process required, among other tasks, the preparation of a light-sensitive emulsion using fresh egg whites, as well as the coating of the glass plate with the liquid just before the exposure was made. The medium became at least one degree more portable with the widening use of the collodion-on-glass process, which eliminated the egg whites.

Photographer unknown. John Thomson with his fiancée (detail from larger photograph), about 1868. John Hillelson–B. S. Kahn Collection, London.

John Thomson, working with the improved process, may have arrived in China as early as 1865.[4] He is probably the most important photographer to have visited China in the nineteenth century and is the only one to have left us a substantial body of work,[5] much of which might not have been preserved had it not been published in the two-volume, *Illustrations of China and Its People*,[6] produced in London between 1872 and 1874. Few of Thomson's original photographs are extant, so we are fortunate that the reproductions were made by the newly invented collotype process, which made possible a large number of facsimile copies of each image on a printing press. The reproductions in the present publication were made directly from Thomson's book.

Thomson possessed a gifted eye, and his work stands with the strongest produced by any photographer of his generation. We are struck by qualities in his images that remove them from the category of mere documentation.

Further, Thomson combined the talents of the portrait photographer and landscapist. He was sensitive to human beings, and he allowed them to project themselves through the photographic image, as in the many portraits of ordinary people that he includes with his portraits of rulers and the landed gentry.

The photographing of anonymous individuals, whether in a street or a studio, was rarely practiced in Thomson's day, owing to the expense of the materials and the time-consuming process of making the picture, and so, as a rule, portraits were made only for those who were willing to pay for the privilege. Subjects drawn from daily life remained important to Thomson, and we find him five years later, upon his return to Europe, publishing a book entitled *Street Life in London*.[7] (Though postdating his pictures of the Chinese, this book is often cited among the earliest published examples of social documentation in photographs.) Thomson excelled as a photographer because he was able to depict eloquently the two sides of China: the variety of the landscape, and the face of its people, a combination not often seen in the work of succeeding photographers, who tended to focus on either the landscape or on the people.

Thomson tells in the introduction to *Illustrations of China and Its People* why he chose the medium of photography:

I hope to see the process which I have thus applied adopted by other travellers; for the faithfulness of such pictures affords the nearest approach that can be made towards placing the reader actually before the scene which is represented.[8]

The reasons for Thomson's attraction to the medium are not essentially different from those of a traveler photographing abroad today.

Reading the text of Thomson's book, one learns a great deal about the history of China at the time of his visit. We read that China was then a nation exploited by outsiders and beset with a weak internal government; we read that there was great antagonism between the ruling Manchu (Mongolian) minority and the Han Chinese; we sense that the yield of the land was insufficient to feed the population; we can hear in Thomson's words, as objective as he was attempting to be, the implication that China was a decadent, ignorant, somewhat barbarian nation. We are told how Westerners addicted the population to opium, which they then imported for sale. We are told about, and shown photographs of, the central business districts of every major Chinese city, populated with structures designed by Western architects and built by outsiders. Thomson's words and pictures portray a nation so fragile in 1870 that change by violent revolution would seem inevitable. It is not an exaggeration to say that Thomson's work constitutes one of the most important examples of photojournalism ever to have been produced, one which even today stands as a model for that kind of reporting.

Thomson was by no means the only photographer in China in the 1870s, but he, like Beato, was among the relatively few Europeans to travel there with the express purpose of making negatives to be taken back to Europe. From the early 1860s there were photographic establishments in the main cities of China that served a different purpose than those of the traveler-photographer. These photographer-shopkeepers, doubtless Westerners, stocked "views," some taken by the man himself, others purloined from photographers like Beato and Thomson, to be sold to travelers. The best of this

Photographer unknown. Stone elephants on the road to the Ming Tombs, about 1870. Private collection, New York.

Photographer unknown. Panorama of Hong Kong, about 1870. John Hillelson–B. S. Kahn Collection, London.

work is very good, but a great deal of it is the result of either insensitive studio setups or thoughtless wandering through the countryside snapping the Chinese in their native habitats. Rarely does one find a name attached to such photographs; the work thus falls into an open-ended category of anonymous commercial photography, a genre that flourished around the world in places favored by tourists.

By 1879 we have a description of one commercial studio in the British colony of Hong Kong that sold stock views to tourists. The photographer's name has not come down to us, but his studio produced the pictures commonly purchased by visitors like Charles I. Lucas, who visited there in 1879.[9] He writes home to his family on March 6 that he was:

up at 8 and finished writing up this letter, then went to photographers to buy views, etc. of Hong Kong, Canton, and Macao.[10]

The photographs Lucas bought that day are preserved in an album compiled upon his return to England. The views of Hong Kong we find in the album are fascinating panoramas that tell us a great deal about the city as it stood at that time, but very little about the sensibility of the photographer except that he had a feeling for the overview. The same can be said for the album's images of peasants in costume posed in the studio: we can see how they dressed and what their faces were like, but precious little can be deduced about the environment from which the people came. Even when the photographer ventured outdoors, people are seen from a distance, with little penetration into the more intimate aspects of their lives. Compared to Thomson's work of a decade earlier, such work is static and unrevealing.

But even commercial photographers in China occasionally made a compelling image. One of the most astonishing photographs in the Lucas album

Photographer unknown. Food vendor with customers, posed in the photographer's studio, about 1875. From the Album of Charles I. Lucas. John Hillelson–B. S. Kahn Collection, London.

is of a beheading ground where we see nothing more than a group of Westerners and a file of beheaded Chinese on the ground. This image was probably the work of a local commercial photographer producing a *memento mori* for the tourist trade. Lucas visited the ground on an off day:

A short time ago the American Consul saw forty-two men's heads cut off in *eight* minutes, by the same man, with swords, so you see he must be a pretty good hand at it. The criminals are arranged in lines of from eight to ten in a row, according to the number, kneeling with their hands tied behind them, the executioner then begins with the front row so that those behind can see how clean their heads will come off when their turn comes. He uses a fresh sword for every five or six heads, a man walks behind him with a supply as he goes along. I regret very much not having seen an execution, it must be an extraordinary sight, very disgusting but worth seeing.

Photographer unknown. Gentlemen at the beheading grounds, about 1879. From the Album of Charles I. Lucas. John Hillelson–B. S. Kahn Collection, London.

Photographer unknown. Edgar Snow with Mao Tse-tung, Pao An, 1936. Lois Wheeler Snow.

Very disgusting but worth seeing! One wonders why he thought it so. Was it because of the sheer spectacle, or was it because the event was a metaphorical drama, so to speak, that shed light on the tone of Chinese society at that point in time? The photograph itself inclines us toward the first interpretation, for we see the Western gentlemen smiling and spirited, as though participating in just one more tourist activity; they are as composed as if they were being photographed astride one of the stone elephants on the road to the Ming Tombs. Could it ever be more appropriate to quote the saying that "one picture is worth a thousand words"?, for on these faces we see written a paradigm of the Western colonialist attitude in China.

By 1890, through the efforts of George Eastman and others, the camera became truly portable, not only through the widespread use of dry, light-

Photographer unknown. C. E. Lucas and his companions on the way to the Ming Tombs, 1911–12. From Album of C. E. Lucas. John Hillelson–B. S. Kahn Collection, London.

Photographer unknown. Nym Wales (Helen Foster Snow) with General Chu Teh, Yenan, Shensi, 1937. Helen Foster Snow.

Helen Foster Snow. Mao Tse-tung, Yenan, Shensi, 1937.

sensitive emulsions on the films, but through the invention of the hand camera. Consequently, between 1890 and 1935 many visitors to China were also amateur photographers. The best of these, like the musician-photographer August Plemenik or Baroness Giovanella Grenier-Caetani,[11] both working at the turn of the century, or Edgar Snow, Nym Wales (Helen Foster Snow), and Perry Atkinson, working in the late 1930s, saw the land with a detached but insightful point of view. Photographs made by talented amateurs, and there are a great many, generally arouse greatest interest when they somehow manage to express a personal point of view, and when the person has access to people or places out of the ordinary, as did the Baroness in her access to the Dowager Empress, and as did Edgar Snow and Nym Wales in their access to the intimate circle of the Communists around Mao Tse-tung.

The Snows, among a handful of trusted Americans, were admitted to the Communists' camp, Edgar to Pao An, Shensi Province, in 1936 and his wife to Yenan, Shensi Province, during late 1936 and 1937.[12] Here they observed Chinese of extraordinary leadership qualities at formative moments in their lives, and saw events not recorded by any other hands. This was one of the most heroic moments China had experienced for centuries, and both the Chinese and the visitors recognized it.

While they were extraordinary journalists, the Snows were not professional photographers. There is little attempt in their snapshots to follow the formal rules of photography. Their photographs are direct and expressive, as in the case of Edgar Snow's portrait of Mao Tse-tung outside the caves at Pao An, shown with near mug-shot directness in full front, profile, and then straight from behind. Equally revealing is Nym Wales'[13] first portrait of Mao Tse-tung, when they met for coffee the day after she arrived in Yenan. Her response is direct and kinetic: she snaps him right across the table and over the coffee can and other utensils in the way. The need for immediacy made formal composition a secondary factor in the creating of the image; composition yielded to candidness. These images indicate how differently amateurs and professionals respond to the picture-taking problem. They lead us to conclude that a talented snapshooter tends to allow the quality of wide-eyed wonder to remain, so that his pictures show the way things really look rather than the way they should look. The professional responds with rationality and control, and tends to idealize his subjects. The best professionals, like Thomson, combine reason with expression; the best amateurs combine instantaneousness with an intuitive sense of composition.

If the work of the talented amateur who has unique access to interesting subjects presents one kind of problem for a historian of photography, the work of the commercial or "staff" photographer presents another set of problems. Some of these have been suggested in our words about the photographs in the album of the elder Lucas. Take, for example, the photograph encountered in the album of the younger Lucas of the meeting of generals Nogi and Stoessel at the surrender of Port Arthur, January 2, 1905. We find them posed here after the Japanese, aided by the Germans, fought the Rus-

Photographer unknown. Generals Stoesel and Nogi at the surrender of Port Arthur, January 2, 1905. From the Album of C. E. Lucas. John Hillelson–B. S. Kahn Collection, London.

Donald Mennie. "By the Hsi Chih Men," plate XX, *The Pageant of Peking*, 1920. Private collection, New York.

sians on Chinese soil. We are entertained by the fact that these men are dressed so quaintly and by the national diversity of their group, which provokes the question of what brought them all together. The question is not answered by the photograph itself, which requires at least the aid of a caption, if not reference to a history book for the full story. Photographically speaking, the question raised is one regarding the kinds of distinctions one can or should make between photographs that are primarily interpretative, such as those by Thomson, the Snows, Cartier-Bresson, and Riboud, and photographs that are meant to be in the most literal sense a document of the moment. The question is complicated by the fact that many photographs of a documentary nature are interesting to look at, and that photographs made for other reasons can be dull. This is to suggest no more than that for one to ask for the motivation behind the making of a photograph is not very productive, and that interesting and informative photographs of China can be found in surprising places.

Among these sources are books published many years ago, such as Donald Mennie's *The Pageant of Peking*, privately published in Shanghai.[14] Although Mennie's name has not come down to us in history books as a photographer of standing, the images in this book are compelling. Mennie probably considered himself an "artistic" photographer, for the image of China generated by his soft-focus photographs is that of a primordial and romantic land.

Falling into the category of photographs taken as historical records alone are a group, presumably by Chinese photographers, documenting important people and events in the early history of the Chinese Communist Party, for example, a blue-print photograph of Mao Tse-tung's first address to the assembled Communist Party.[15] Simply as a photograph, it tells us little, for we cannot recognize the identity of the man, or even get a sense for the event in progress without reading the caption in Chinese printed across the top. The picture is faint, with an odd blue tone to the image, stained, folded, and wrinkled. The principal values here are not photographic, and no such line of thinking can make the images into any more than the work of a commercial photographer attempting to get his picture under very difficult circumstances. Such pictures are precious as documents of Chinese history, but they are of marginal value photographically, in spite of being interesting as objects.

Mao Tse-tung addressing the Congress of the Chinese Communist Party, 1935.

Photographers unknown. From the collection of Edgar Snow.

Chinese Soldiers, about 1935.

Robert Capa. Evans Fordyce Carlson with his equipment in China, 1937. Magnum Photos, New York.

Photographer unknown. John Ferno, Joris Ivens, and Robert Capa, at Battle of Taierhchwang, 1938. Magnum Photos, New York.

A similar response is generated by a group portrait outdoors of ranking Communist officials. The image is faded, stained, and quartered by three transverse folds. With some surprise, one finds that a handful of the figures have been made illegible by the addition of painted strokes resembling flames. This odd manipulation of the photograph, unabashed censorship, again arouses one's curiosity, although the response is to nonphotographic values. Such an image, straddling the line between bald documentation and surrealism, underscores the fineness of the line between the conventional categories of photography.

By 1938, the numbers of tourists to China dwindled to a small number as a result of the civil war, which had been burning with varying degrees of heat since 1927. Most of the photographs extant from the period between 1935 and 1948 were by persons either attached to the U.S. military or by war correspondents representing the foreign press. Evans Fordyce Carlson,[16] a U.S. Marine attached as an observer in the Communist camp, assumed a role similar to that of the Snows: that of the guest invited into a rarely visited home. His photographs are descriptive of the military aspect of Communist life, but they fail to penetrate into the private lives of the principals in the way the Snows' pictures do. In attitude they fall between that of the professional objectively recording the event, and that of the inspired amateur.

Robert Capa[17] was in China at the same time as Edgar and Helen Snow, Evans Carlson, and Perry Atkinson. While the others were visiting in the homes of the Chinese Communist elite, Capa was on the battlefield seeing the country from the point of view of the rifleman. Compare Capa's situation with Perry Atkinson's,[18] an American businessman who took many photographs. The air raids on Nanking by the Japanese meant business as usual for him. Atkinson writes in his diary for August 21, 1937:

Slept 3 hours before air raid 4:15–7:00 a.m.; full red moon setting, bright stars and daylight 4:45; saw 3 japs shot at 5:15 & chinese repulsing 5:30; fell asleep 6: & raid over 7; up 8 to tea, shave, bath, breakfast & out at 8:30 but caught in 2nd raid 8:30–9:00; out rickshaw office 9:30; terminated my inspection of C. T. del'y receipts & records w/suggestions for improving filing, control by reforming "chit-book", and cross reference in C. T. records; coffee & checked prices rest of morning—then took April invoices home w/me to hotel at 1:30; tiffin w/sung & aviators 1:40–2:15, chatted war w/aviators till 3; & up for siesta and check prices until 5:30 . . .

Evans Fordyce Carlson (?). From the collection of Evans Fordyce Carlson. Evans C. Carlson.

Young Communists in the creative ranks. Left to right: Auyang (dramatist), Liu (novelist), King (journalist), Lin San (poet), and Wang Yang (photographer), 1937.

Children, Hopei, 1937.

Students at the Red Army Academy, Yenan, 1937.

Perry Atkinson. From his scrapbook of views around Shanghai, 1937. Karlyn Atkinson.

Photographer unknown. Perry Atkinson, 1937.

Atkinson responded sensitively but somewhat passively with his camera, focusing on those aspects of the life around him that were either quaint or for other reasons provocative. On the other hand, Robert Capa, like Felice Beato half a century earlier, was happy only when he was in the thick of battle. The photographs of Capa and Atkinson, originating from such different experiences, are barely comparable.

Henri Cartier-Bresson, Marc Riboud, and René Burri, in China at various intervals between 1948 and the present, were among the few Westerners who succeeded in obtaining visas to visit China for the express purpose of photography. Each went knowing his pictorial record would be one of the few disseminated to the Western world. Added to this burden was the complicating open-endedness of their assignments: to record all of China and its people for the eyes of Westerners. Paradoxically, in spite of the fact that they are professionals, the three were also tourists and responded like any tourist, photographing what caught their eyes, and what they felt would be revealing to viewers thousands of miles away. They were not lucky enough to have the delimiting geographical framework of Yenan that the Snows had, nor could they focus only on the obvious motifs that attract the average photographer-traveler: the monuments, architecture, and natives caught in characteristic settings. Nor by any means was it as simple as for the commercial or studio photographer, who photographed only what he was asked by someone else to do, or what he was able on his own initiative to set up in his studio. The European visitors were given the responsibility of characterizing an entire nation, one which had grown unaccustomed to receiving Western visitors.

Henri Cartier-Bresson [19] has had the longest association with China of the three. It began with a visit there as a young man with his father. By happy accident he was in China during the last days of the civil war in 1948–49 as a war correspondent. He witnessed the last five months of the Kuomintang government of Chiang Kai-shek, and the first six months of Mao Tse-tung's Communist regime. During that stay he recorded what was symbolically the transition from the old China to the new. He was able to return again in 1958 to record how the "new" China actually fulfilled the promises it made the people at its birth in 1949.

Cartier-Bresson has called himself a "street photographer." In this description he expresses in words what is clear in his photographs: that he is interested in photographing people engaged in their everyday activities.

Cartier-Bresson found this more difficult to accomplish in China, where candid photography of people on the streets is considered more an invasion of privacy than it is in his native France. Cartier-Bresson's photographs might be likened to the lithographs of Honoré Daumier from the 1840s to the extent that both strive to penetrate to the essence of their subject by capturing it at the most characteristically revealing moment, called by Cartier-Bresson "the decisive moment."

Cartier-Bresson's achievement in recording the events of 1948–49 can be well appreciated only after a moment's thought on the nature of the events themselves: the Nationalist government failing, a new, radically different political force perched ready to prevail, failure of the currency, interruption of the food supply. Cartier-Bresson's task was to find the "decisive moment" within a state of chaos. If the photographs from his visit of 1958 seem less tense, less charged with emotion than those of 1948–49, it is because the times and the state of mind of the people had also changed.

Cartier-Bresson has, in some way or another, influenced the course of photojournalism in the twentieth century as much as any other photographer. Marc Riboud[20] considers him a friend and mentor. In spite of their close personal relationship, Riboud's photographs express a sensibility quite different from that of Cartier-Bresson. While Cartier-Bresson focuses on people as people, Riboud is more moved by people in their environments. Riboud consistently sees people in a spatial context and attempts where possible to make the layers of space play against one another, much in the manner of a Dutch baroque etcher, as in his photograph of two peasant women hoeing a field. In other cases he sets up a dynamic relationship between figure and background, as in his photograph of figures moving in one direction while figures on a poster move in the opposite direction. Unlike Cartier-Bresson, Riboud is interested in landscape as a genre unto itself, and he attempts, like his colleague René Burri,[21] to evoke the most lyrical aspects of the Chinese countryside when he encounters them. Riboud has a sense of direct composition that is almost schematic and oriented to the center of the image; in contrast, Cartier-Bresson strives toward imbalance generated by tensional elements at the edges of his photographs.

Examining this anthology of photographs of China, one might ask what it contributes to our knowledge of photography. For one thing, it permits us to test the work of a major nineteenth-century figure, John Thomson, against some by major twentieth-century figures. Thomson, even when he was trying hardest, failed to achieve an intimate penetration into the everyday lives of his subjects; the best photographs of twentieth-century China succeed where he failed. On the other hand, rarely do twentieth-century photographers match Thomson in the realm of formal portraiture, as in his studies of the Chinese aristocracy.

Going further, our book juxtaposes work by nonprofessionals and acknowledged masters. This raises questions about the nature of the medium, many of which have yet to be resolved. Thrown into perspective are photography's multiple roles: as vehicle of communication, as mnemonic device, as medium for artistic expression. We are left to conclude that the best snapshots by nonprofessionals possess an intimacy and directness shared by naïve artists in any medium, tackling any subject. The best work by professionals is objective and descriptive, yet it also shows awareness of visual form, and a consistent personal aesthetic. There is little sense of personal style in the snapshot or documentary photographs, and whatever fascination these images hold is generally derived from qualities inherent in the medium itself.

Cumulatively, the photographs carry information about China otherwise difficult to convey. We can see a nation that clearly went through a century of warfare, both internal and external; we see that the Chinese today dress more as they did in the nineteenth century than Westerners do; we can see above all else that for a century China had to contend with the presence of aggressive and energetic Westerners. The late photographs by Riboud and Burri show a nation beginning to be at one with itself and the rest of the world. They are evidence that the political *rapprochement* of 1971, which inspired the Museum's exhibition and now this book, was neither accident nor whim, but the result of natural growth.

Weston J. Naef
May, 1972

NOTES

[1] There exist at least two scrapbooks in private hands of calotypes (talbotypes) made in India in the early 1850s.

[2] Helmut and Alison Gernsheim, *The History of Photography*, London, rev. ed., 1969, pp. 293–303.

[3] *Ibid.*, pp. 270–271.

[4] *Ibid.*, pp. 288–289. Thomson was born in Edinburgh, which was an early center for the practice of photography, thanks to the pioneering efforts of D. O. Hill and Robert

Adamson, who practiced W. F. Talbot's calotype process and taught it to many persons around Edinburgh. Thomson's early work may have been as an architectural photographer, as is suggested by the illustrations to Cuthbert Bede's *The Visitor's Handbook to Rosslyn and Hawthornden*, Edinburgh (about 1864), which the author credits in a note to one J. Thomson. A unique album of original photographs by Thomson of areas in the Far East other than China is in the Arnold Crane Collection, Chicago.

5 The general working procedure of photographers in the 1870s is explained in the first English edition of Gaston Tissandier's *A History and Handbook of Photography*, London, 1876, which was edited by John Thomson.

6 Weston J. Naef, "John Thomson's *Illustrations of China and Its People*," *The Metropolitan Museum of Art Bulletin*, February–March, 1972, pp. 194–195. Thomson's other books on the Far East are: *The Antiquities of Gambodia* (sic), London, 1875; *The Straits of Malacca, Indo-China, and China: or Ten Years' Travels, Adventures and Residence Abroad*, London, 1876, and *Through China with a Camera*, Westminster, 1898.

7 Robert Doty, "John Thomson's *Street Life in London*," *Image*, no. 56. Thomson's book was reissued in 1969 by Benjamin Blom, New York and London, with a publisher's note re-emphasizing the merit of the text by Adolphe Smith.

8 Further commentary by Thomson regarding his use of the camera as a tool is found in the preface to *Through China with a Camera*.

9 Charles I. Lucas visited China as one stop on a voyage around the world. His son, C. E. Lucas, was to make a similar journey in 1911–12. The albums of photographs from both visits, as well as a transcription of C. I. Lucas' letters and journals, are in the John Hillelson–B. S. Kahn Collection, London.

10 Charles I. Lucas, Diary and Letters, as transcribed by his mother into a notebook.

11 August Plemenik and Baroness Giovanella Grenier-Caetani were represented in an exhibition at the Hallmark Gallery, New York, "Four Cameras in China, Then and Now," March 9–May 18, 1972, organized by Margaret Weiss.

12 Edgar Snow (1905–72), born in Missouri, went to the Far East at the age of twenty-two. He lectured at Yenching University and studied the language and culture of the country. He served as correspondent for a number of magazines and newspapers including the *Chicago Tribune*, *New York Sun*, and *New York Herald Tribune*. His intimate acquaintance with the Chinese Communists in 1936 provided him with material to write the classic work on the origins of Communist China, *Red Star Over China*, 1937. He followed this with numerous books on China. Thanks to his rapport with Mao Tse-tung, he was the only American to obtain a travel visa from the People's Republic of China and to have the U.S. government's permission to travel in a region proscribed to American citizens; he visited there under these arrangements in 1960, 1964–65, and 1970.

13 Helen Foster (Nym Wales) arrived in China in 1932 as a secretary at the American Consulate in Shanghai. She met Edgar Snow there and they were married in Tokyo on Christmas Day, 1932. She wrote several books on China under the pseudonym of Nym Wales, among them *Inside Red China*, New York, Doubleday, 1939, and *Red Dust*, Stanford, 1952 (reprinted with additions as *The Chinese Communists*, Westport, Greenwood Press, 1972).

14 Donald Mennie, *The Pageant of Peking*, Shanghai, 1920, with introduction by Putnam Weale, and sixty-six gravure illustrations.

15 These photographs from the earliest moments of the Chinese Communist government were among the few to survive the "Long March," and were given to Edgar Snow as sources for his book *Red Star Over China*. They were made on blueprint paper from ordinary negatives in the absence of conventional photographic printing papers.

16 Evans Fordyce Carlson (1896–1947) was in China at various intervals for over a decade, beginning in 1926. In 1937, a captain in the Marines, he served as observer for the Navy, both on the Nationalist and Communist sides. His experience led to the formation of "Carlson's Raiders" in World War II, whose personnel were trained in the principles of guerrilla warfare taught at the Red Army Academy, Yenan. In China, Carlson was concerned primarily with understanding military organization and strategy, and used photography as an adjunct to other note-taking. His unpublished diary contains candid observations upon many of the leaders, both Nationalist and Communist.

17 Robert Capa (1913–54) photographed five wars and earned himself the reputation of being one of the finest war correspondents of the twentieth century. He died, the casualty of a land mine, in 1954 in Indo-China. Many of his photographs of China were first published in *Life*, IV, no. 20 (May 16, 1938), and later in *Images of War*, Grossman Publishers, New York, 1964.

18 Perry Atkinson (1902–62) was a compulsive traveler to remote regions of the world. He was an explorer in the old sense of the word, seeking unmapped regions both for the sake of the visit and to search for natural resources to fill the needs of industry. He spent the years between 1931 and 1941 in the Far East, and while in China studied the Shanghai and Peking dialects.

19 Henri Cartier-Bresson (b. 1908) has for over forty years been recognized as a master of photography used as a narrative and documentary vehicle. His work on China has been widely published, notably in a collaborative effort with Jean-Paul Sartre, *D'une Chine a l'autre*, Paris, 1954, and in collaboration with Barbara Brakeley Miller, *China*, New York, 1964.

20 Marc Riboud (b. 1923), a French free-lance photographer, visited China in 1957, 1965, and 1971. His photographs have been published along with a text by him in the book *Three Banners of China*, New York, 1966.

21 René Burri (b. 1933), a Swiss photographer and film-maker, spent several months traveling through China in 1965, from which emerged a film, The Two Faces of China, as well as a body of still photographs.

JOHN THOMSON

My design in the accompanying work is to present a series of pictures of China and its people, such as shall convey an accurate impression of the country I traversed as well as of the arts, usages, and manners which prevail in different provinces of the Empire. With this intention I made the camera the constant companion of my wanderings, and to it I am indebted for the faithful reproduction of the scenes I visited, and of the types of race with which I came into contact.

Those familiar with the Chinese and their deeply-rooted superstitions will readily understand that the carrying out of my task involved both difficulty and danger. In some places there were many who had never yet set eyes upon a pale-faced stranger; and the literati, or educated classes, had fostered a notion amongst such as these, while evil spirits of every kind were carefully to be shunned, none ought to be so strictly avoided as the "Fan Qui" or "Foreign Devil," who assumed human shape, and appeared solely for the furtherance of his own interests, often owing the success of his undertakings to an ocular power, which enabled him to discover the hidden treasures of heaven and earth. I therefore frequently enjoyed the reputation of being a dangerous geomancer, and my camera was held to be a dark mysterious instrument, which, combined with my naturally, or supernaturally, intensified eyesight gave me power to see through rocks and mountains, to pierce the very souls of the natives, and to produce miraculous pictures by some black art, which at the same time bereft the individual depicted of so much of the principle of life as to render his death a certainty within a very short period of years.

Accounted, for these reasons, the forerunner of death, I found portraits of children difficult to obtain, while, strange as it may be thought in a land where filial piety is esteemed the highest of virtues, sons and daughters brought their aged parents to be placed before the foreigner's silent and mysterious instrument of destruction. The trifling sums that I paid for the privilege of taking such subjects would probably go to help in the purchase of a coffin, which, conveyed ceremoniously to the old man's house, would there be deposited to await the hour of dissolution, and the body of the parent whom his son had honoured with the gift. Let none of my readers suppose that I am speaking in jest. To such an extreme pitch has the notion of honouring ancestors with due mortuary rites been carried in China, that an affectionate parent would regard children who should present him with a cool and comfortable coffin as having begun in good time to display the duty and respect which every well-regulated son and daughter is expected to bestow.

The superstitious influences, such as I have described, rendered me a frequent object of mistrust, and led to my being stoned and roughly handled on more occasions than one. It is, however, in and about large cities that the wide-spread hatred of foreigners is most conspicuously displayed. In many of the country districts, and from officials who have been associated with Europeans, and who therefore appreciate the substantial benefits which foreign intercourse can confer, I have met with numerous tokens of kindness, and a hospitality as genuine as could be shown to a stranger in any part of the world.

It is a novel experiment to attempt to illustrate a book of travels with photographs, a few years back so perishable, and so difficult to reproduce. But the art is now so far advanced, that we can multiply the copies with the same facility, and print them with the same materials as in the case of woodcuts or engravings. I feel somewhat sanguine about the success of the undertaking, and I hope to see the process which I have thus applied adopted by other travellers; for the faithfulness of such pictures affords the nearest approach that can be made towards placing the reader actually before the scene which is represented.

The letter-press which accompanies the pictures, and which will render them, as I trust, more interesting and more intelligible, is compiled from information derived from the most trustworthy sources, as well as from notes either made by me at the time the subjects were taken, or gathered during a residence of nearly five years in China.

I have endeavoured to arrange these notes and illustrations as far as possible in the natural order or sequence of my journeys, which extended over a distance, estimated roughly, of between 4,000 and 5,000 miles.

I shall start from the British colony of Hong-Kong, once said to be the grave of Europeans, but which now, with its city of Victoria, its splendid public buildings, parks and gardens, its docks, factories, telegraphs and fleets of steamers, may be fairly considered the birthplace of a new era in eastern civilization. I will next proceed by the Pearl river to Canton, the city above all others possessing the greatest historical interest to foreigners, as the scene of their early efforts to gain a footing in the country. Thence I will cross to Formosa, an island which, by its tropical luxuriance and by the grandeur of its mountain scenery, deserves the name "Isla Formosa" which the early Portuguese voyagers conferred upon it. At Taiwan the ruin of the old fort Zelandia will be found both curious and interesting; it was the stronghold from which Koksinga, the famous Chinese adventurer, succeeded in driving the Dutch, some of whom are said to have sought shelter among the aborigines, who still possess old Dutch documents, and have traditions about the doings of their kind-hearted, red-haired brothers. This island is daily rising in importance, as the recent development of its resources is fostering a growing trade at the open ports, and it is destined to play a leading part in the future as one of the great coal-fields of China.

Crossing to the mainland, I will visit Swatow and Chow-chow-fu, noted for the quality of their sugar and rice, for their turbulent clans, and for village wars that remind one of the feudal times of Scotland.

I shall then pass northward to Amoy, one of the first ports visited by foreigners, remarkable in modern times as that part of the Fukien province from which a constant tide of emigration flows to the Straits of Malacca and to America, and noticeable also for the independent character of its people, as among the last who succumbed to the Tartar yoke. The river Min will here afford examples of the grand mountain scenery to be found in the Fukien province, and will form an attractive portion of the work, as the great artery which carries an annual supply of about seventy million pounds of tea to the Foochow market.

Following the route northward the reader will next be introduced to Shanghai, the greatest of the treaty ports of China, where, within a few years, a foreign settlement has sprung up, on the banks of the Woosang, of such vast proportions, as to lead a visitor to fancy that he has been suddenly transported to one of our great English ports; the crowd of shipping, the wharves, warehouses, and landing-stages, the stone embankment, the elegance and costliness of the buildings, the noise of constant traffic in the streets, the busy roads, smooth as a billiard-table, and the well-kept garden that skirts the river affording evidence of foreign taste and refinement, all tending to aid the illusion. One has only, however, to drive beyond the foreign settlement to dispel the dream, and to find the native dwellings huddled

JOHN THOMSON

together, as if pressed back to make way for the higher civilization that has planted a city in their midst. Leaving Shanghai, I will proceed to Ningpo and Snowy Valley, the favourite spring resort of Shanghai residents, and justly celebrated for the beauty of its azaleas, its mountain scenery, its cascades and waterfalls; thence to the Yangtsze Kiang, visiting *en route* the treaty ports and the ancient capital, Nanking, passing through the weird scenery of the gorges of the Upper Yangtsze, and penetrating as far as Kweichow-fu. The concluding journey will embrace Chefoo, the Peiho, Tientsin and Peking. The remarkable antiquities, the palace, temples, and observatory; the different races in the great metropolis; the ruins of the Summer Palace and the Ming Tombs shall be presented to the reader: after which I will guide him through the Nankow Pass, and take my leave of him at the Great Wall.

(Introduction to his *Illustrations of China and Its People*, London, 1873–74.)

John Thomson's photographs are reproduced from the Metropolitan Museum's copy of *Illustrations of China and Its People* (Elisha Whittelsey Fund, 1971.635.1–2.) The captions have been adapted from Thomson's text.

CAPTIONS

1 *Prince Kung.* About forty years of age in 1870, Kung was the sixth son of Emperor Tao Kwang, who reigned from 1820 to 1850. Prior to 1860 Kung was little known beyond the precincts of the court. However, when the emperor fled the Summer Palace, it was Kung who came forward to meet the ministers of the Allied Powers and negotiate the conditions of peace.

2 *Physic Street, Canton.* The streets of a Chinese city differ greatly from those of Europe, and are always extremely narrow, except at Nanking and Peking. They are paved with slabs of stone, usually worn down by the traffic to a hollow in the center of the path, and this disagreeable substitute for the gutters of European thoroughfares forms the only means by which the rain water is carried off.

3 *The cangue.* The cangue, or collar of wood, is one of the lighter punishments of China, inflicted for minor offenses, such as petty theft. The nature of the crime, as well as the name and residence of the delinquent, if he has any, are described in prominent characters on cards, and fixed to the cangue. The wearer is usually located in front of the house or shop where the offense was committed, and is forced to depend for food on the charity of passers-by.

4 *A tea-tasting room, Canton.* Three tea merchants in a foreign taster's room await an offer for their samples. Every foreign house in Canton that does any trade in tea has a room especially fitted up for the accommodation of the taster. The windows of the room have a northern aspect, and are screened off, so as to admit only a steady sky-light, which falls directly on the teaboard beneath. Upon this board the samples are spread in square wooden trays, and it is under the uniform light above described that the minute inspection of color, make, and external appearance of the leaves takes place.

5 *Four heads, types of the laboring class.* The two upper ones are fair types of the aged laborers of China. Darby and Joan have for many years been associated together, and their life has been a uniform scene of hardships and toil. Two generations have now grown up around them, and their sons and grandsons have succeeded them as the bread-winners of the family. The old man, venerated as the head of the family, gratifies his taste for information by spelling through the cheap literature of the day. This commonly consists of what to us would appear tedious and uninteresting tales, which appeal greatly to the credulity of the reader. The old woman still busies herself in the lighter domestic duties; she is skillful with her needle, and invaluable as a nurse in time of sickness. The two lower heads are those of a son and daughter; they belong to the same class.

6 *The abbott and monks of Kushan Monastery.* It is interesting to note how closely the dress of the Buddhist monk resembles the monastic garb of ancient Europe. In both we see a robe, long, simple, and ample, falling loosely to the feet; and both carry a cowl for the protection of the head in cold weather, as well as a rosary to aid the wearer in keeping his debtor and creditor account of good and bad thoughts, words, and works.

7 *A Canton junk.* The term junk, applied by Europeans to all Chinese craft, whether trading vessels or ships of war, is probably derived from "jung," the Javanese word for a large boat. Chinese ships vary in dimensions, model, and appearance in the different parts of the Empire as much as do the sailing craft of Europe. The vessel under sail on the left is a coasting trader of Kwangtung build, and may be regarded as one of the clipper fleet of Southern China. It looks heavy and unhandy, but it will make good sailing with a fair wind. The hull is strengthened and held together by massive hard-wood beams or girders, sweeping in a triple row from stem to stern. The hold is divided into watertight compartments, so that were an injury sustained, and one or more compartments filled with water, the vessel might still have buoyancy left to float ashore or into dock.

8 *Wu-shan Gorge, Province of Szechuan.* Wu-shan Gorge, which we entered on the morning of February 18, 1871, is more than twenty miles in length. The Yangtsze here was perfectly placid, and the view which met our gaze at the mouth of the gorge was perhaps the finest of its kind that we had encountered. The mountains rose in confused masses to a great altitude, while the most distant peak at the extremity of the reach resembled a cut sapphire, its snow lines spar-

JOHN THOMSON

kling in the sun like the gleams of light on the facets of a gem. The other cliffs and precipices gradually deepened in hue until they reached the bold lights and shadows of the rock foreground.

9 *The Clock Tower, Hong Kong.* Designed by Mr. Rawlings in 1861, the tower is a great ornament to the city, and the clock too, when regulated properly, is of no inconsiderable service. The tower is seen to advantage from the harbor, and the lighted dial of the clock forms a good landmark to guide the benighted steersman to the landing steps at peddlar's wharf. On the left, and nearest to the tower, stands the Hong Kong Hotel, constructed after the model of the large hotels in London. The turbaned figure on the right is an Indian policeman, of whom there were at one time about 300 in the force. They are now being gradually drafted off to India, and replaced by Europeans and West-Indian Negroes.

10 *One of the city guard, Peking.* The subject is a Tartar bannerman, Old Wang. Wrapped in his sheep-skin coat, and in an underclothing of rags, he lay through the cold nights on the stone step of the outer gateway, and only roused himself at times to answer the call of his fellow-watchman near at hand. This call is supposed to be passed from watchman to watchman all round the city. Wang employed also a wooden clapper to let the inmates of the house know he was astir, and to scare away thieves.

1 *Prince Kung, 1870–72*

JOHN THOMSON

2 *Physic Street, Canton, 1870–72*

4 *Tea tasting room, Canton, 1870–72*

3 *The cangue, 1870–72*

JOHN THOMSON

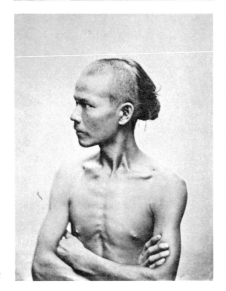

5　*Four heads, 1870–72*

6 *Kushan Monastery, 1870–72*

JOHN THOMSON

7   *A Canton junk, 1870–72*

8 *Wu-shan Gorge, Szechuan, 1870–72*

JOHN THOMSON

9 *The clock tower, Hong-Kong, 1870–72*

10 *Old Wang, Peking, 1870–72*

JOHN THOMSON

EDGAR SNOW

During my seven years in China, hundreds of questions have been asked about the Chinese Red Army, the Soviets and the Communist movement. The fact was that there had been perhaps no greater mystery among nations, no more confused an epic, than the story of Red China. Fighting in the very heart of the most populous nation on earth, the Celestial Reds had for nine years been isolated by a news blockade as effective as a stone fortress. A wall of thousands of enemy troops constantly surrounded them; their territory was more inaccessible than Tibet. No one had voluntarily penetrated that wall and returned to write of his experiences since the first Chinese Soviet was established in southeastern Hunan, in November, 1927.

Then in June, 1936, a close Chinese friend of mine brought me news of . . . a situation which was later to culminate in the sensational kidnaping of Generalissimo Chiang Kai-shek, and to change the current of Chinese history. . . . I learned with this news of a possible method of entry to Red territory. . . . The opportunity was unique and not to be missed. I decided to take it, and attempt to break a news blockade nine years old. . . . I had little to cheer me on my way. Nothing, in truth, but a letter of introduction to Mao Tse-tung, chairman of the Soviet Government. . . . I met Mao soon after my arrival: a gaunt, rather Lincolnesque figure, above average height for a Chinese, somewhat stooped, with a head of thick black hair grown very long, and with large, searching eyes, a high-bridged nose and prominent cheekbones. My fleeting impression was of an intellectual face of great shrewdness . . .[1]

I was the first person to penetrate a civil war blockade and interview and photograph Mao Tse-tung, Chou En-lai and other leaders of the old Chinese Red Army. That was a century ago (1936), the Communists and the Nationalists under Chiang Kai-shek called a truce in their first nine years of mutual extermination, in order to compete in a war of resistance against Japan.

Mao Tse-tung told me his own story and the history of the Chinese Communist revolution up to that time, which appeared in my book *Red Star Over China*, first published in 1937. A Chinese version of that book came out before the English edition and provided countless Chinese with the first authentic information about Chinese Communists. Among those readers were many youths whom I have met again as second-or-third echelon leaders of Red China.

This background made it possible for me to be given a welcome, despite official hostility between Peking and Washington, when I returned to China in 1960 for the first time since the end of the Second World War. Relatively few of the small number of occidentals who have seen Red China ever lived there before the revolution. I believe I was, among resident American correspondents who knew China in pre-war days, the first to return.[2]

[1] *Red Star Over China*, 1937; quoted from preface to revised edition, Grove Press, New York, 1968.
[2] *Red China Today*, 1962; quoted from revised edition, Random House, New York, 1971.

1   *Mao Tse-tung addressing the People's
Liberation Army, Pao-An, 1936.*

EDGAR SNOW

2–4 *Mao Tse-tung, Pao-An, 1936.*

5 *Mao Tse-tung with Ho Tzu-ch'en, Pao-An, 1936.*

EDGAR SNOW

III

NYM WALES (Helen Foster Snow)

I went to Yenan in 1937 and spent over five months there, four in the city itself. Of course, I never would have attempted such an adventure except that I was exempt from Chinese law. Nevertheless, I went against a military order proscribing travel there. It was necessary for me to climb out of a window at night from my room with the help of two sympathetic sons of missionaries. During those months in Yenan I took several hundred photographs and made notes for three books.

Being in Yenan at that particular moment was an extraordinary experience because the Communist leaders had assembled themselves there all together for the first time in order to organize their campaign against Japan. My primary objective was to record the biographies of the most important figures, a great number of whom were later to assume positions of importance in the Communist government after 1949.

There were several others in the Red areas besides my husband Edgar Snow and me. Among them were Jim Bertram, Rewi Alley, and Evans Carlson. Edgar was assembling notes for what was to become the classic book on the formation of the Chinese Communist government, *Red Star Over China*. Rewi Alley brought the industrial revolution to the Chinese villages by introducing the idea of craft cooperatives, and Evans Carlson contributed the experience and know-how of the U.S. Marines, as well as accumulating notes for his own book on the period, *Twin Stars of China*.

We all knew we were witnessing history-making events, and I don't think it is wrong to describe us as a group of pilgrims in search of truth and facts.

January, 1972

CAPTIONS

1 Yenan with the Yen River, 1937.

2 Po Ku, Chou En-lai, Chu Teh, Mao Tse-tung, Yenan, 1937.

3 General Chou En-lai, Yenan, 1937.

4 Soldiers with posters adapted from photographs of Stalin, Lenin, and Mao Tse-tung, Yenan, 1937.

5 Hsu Meng-ch'iu, historian of the early Communist Chinese Party.

6 General Chu Teh addressing the troops in Yenan, 1937.

7 Red Army Academy graduates marching off to fight the Japanese, Yenan, 1937.

8 Red Army Academy students drilling, Yenan, 1937.

9 Lolo tribesmen recruited during the Long March, at the Communist Party School for Minorities, Yenan, 1937.

10 Soldiers of the People's Liberation Army in review, Yenan, 1937.

11 Youthful army buglers, Yenan, 1937.

12 Members of the dramatics corps at practice, Yenan, 1937.

13 Young soldier called "Little Devil" (Hsiao Kuei), Yenan, 1937.

14 Ho Ta-ch'ing, army orderly, Yenan, 1937.

15 Constance Chang, Huang Hua (first ambassador to the United Nations from the People's Republic of China), and Ch'en Han-p'o at Yenching University, 1936.

16 Huang Ching (Yu Ch'i-wei) addressing student rally, Peking, December 16, 1936.

1 *Yenan with the Yen River, 1937*

NYM WALES

2 *Po Ku, Chou En-lai, Chu Teh, Mao Tse-tung, Yenan, 1937*

3 *General Chou En-lai, Yenan, 1937*

4 *Yenan, 1937*

5 *Hsu Meng-ch'iu, Yenan, 1937*

6 General Chu Teh, Yenan, 1937

NYM WALES

7–10   *Yenan, 1937*

11–14 *Youthful communists, Yenan, 1937*

NYM WALES

15 *Constance Chang, Huang Hua, and Ch'en Han-p'o,*
Yenching University, 1936

16 *Huang Ching (Yu Ch'i-wei), Peking, 1936*

IV

ROBERT CAPA

Many peoples are represented in the huge Chinese nation. But all these peoples seem to be formed and bound together by something which so far has resisted even the heaviest storms of our times. One could get used to it and remember that almost every Chinese, even the most modern in his beliefs, has his roots in a time which is far removed from our bloody present. We Europeans also, who have invented all these arms and war machines, do not live only amidst the noise of battle.

I think I realized for the first time what is special about these people when I met the columns of the lightly wounded: slowly they marched by, single file, with bandages on their arms, their heads, their eyes, or their necks. Silent rows of men who had come from one of the heaviest battles in thousands of years of Chinese history. Surely many of them had seen terrible things, had passed horrible hours, days or weeks. But all terror had passed from their faces. Their fresh wounds must have hurt them—yet in their faces there was nothing of the tension with which European wounded fight to suppress their pain. They marched by calmly, almost indifferent to their own pain.

War is a task which one is irrevocably faced with; but it doesn't require any big illusion to cause a Chinese to give up his life. All this bears only remote resemblance to nationalism in the European sense of the word. The idea of nationalism which has begun to form in China during these last decades is at the same time less definite and more comprehensive than that of a European. Thus the Chinese will to stem the attack has an Asiatic depth and limitlessness.

Just think how much it may mean one day when this Chinese initiative will be used for tasks other than to resist the brunt of enemy attack.

(from Letters, 1938)

CAPTIONS 1 A fifteen-year-old stands at attention before his company leaves for the front and the decisive Sino-Japanese battles of the year. Hankow, March, 1938.

2 A woman mourns her husband, killed in the battle of Taierhchwang. April, 1938.

3 Air raid. Hankow, 1938.

4 Hankow, 1938.

5 His own garden provides this man with an air raid shelter. Hankow, 1938.

6–9 Air raid, Hankow, April 19, 1938. In honor of Emperor Hirohito's thirty-seventh birthday, Japanese generals sent fifty planes to bomb Hankow. The planes were met by twenty-three Chinese planes. For an hour, a fierce battle ensued. In the photographs we see people first with expressions of fear, followed by curiosity, then joy and pride as the Chinese gun down Japanese planes.

10 After incendiary bombardments, a woman tries futilely to extinguish the fire. Hankow, 1938.

11 A wounded soldier treks six miles to a hospital behind the front lines after the Chinese victory at Taierhchwang. April, 1938.

12 After the bombardments, this mother is one of many who keep alive by eating herbs and roots. Taierhchwang, 1938.

13 Mme. Chiang Kai-shek caring for the wounded. Hankow, 1938. Formerly Mei-ling Soong, Mme. Chiang was educated in the United States. Through her influence many Western attitudes were introduced into China.

14 Chiang Kai-shek presides over his Supreme War Council just prior to the departure of the twenty-eight German advisors who had been instrumental in training his army. Hankow, July 4, 1938.

15 University students training as soldiers. Canton, 1938.

16 Departure of Chiang Kai-shek's German military advisors. Hankow, July 5, 1938.

1 *Hankow, 1938*

ROBERT CAPA

2 *Taierhchwang, 1938*

3 *Hankow, 1938*

4 Hankow, 1938

5 Hankow, 1938

ROBERT CAPA

6–9 Hankow, 1938

ROBERT CAPA

10 *Hankow, 1938*

11 *Taierhchwang, 1938*

ROBERT CAPA

12 *Taierhchwang, 1938*

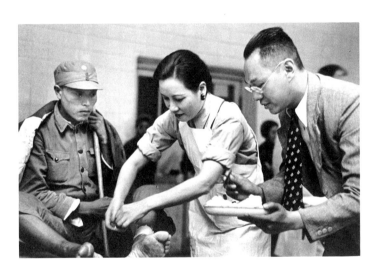

13 *Hankow, 1938*

14 *Hankow, 1938*

ROBERT CAPA

15 *Canton, 1938*

16 *Hankow, 1938*

ROBERT CAPA

V

HENRI CARTIER-BRESSON

In 1958, three days before I took the plane to China, I showed my visa to a waiter in a Chinese restaurant in Paris. To my great surprise, he informed me that my papers, instead of authorizing me to enter China six days later, June 17, would expire on that very date. All the same, I finally arrived on June 16, and fortunately my visa was extended.

To the authorities, who received me very politely, I presented my desires: having lived in China nine years earlier during the last six months of the Kuomintang and the first six months of the People's Republic of China, I hoped that my camera would be able to record the changes. Through my photographs I especially wanted to establish the rapport between that which remained of the ancient society, particularly in evidence in remote areas, and the actual transformations—the factories, the agricultural cooperatives, the new conception of men and women, and so on. I also just wanted to stroll through the streets.

These desires drew me across China for nearly four months. From Peking I went to Manchuria (now called the Northwest Province), then to a great dam being built on the Yellow River, the Suman Tia. Then I stayed in Lanchow, springboard of the development of China's West, and on to Yumen, the petroleum center in the Gobi Desert. All of my trip across China was made by train, with the exception of a plane flight from Yumen to Uramachi, the capital of Sinkiang. From the oasis of Turfan I returned to the East. I traveled to Sian, one of the ancient capitals, to Chongtu, and on to Chungking. From there I spent three days in a boat descending the Yangtsze gorges to Wuhan. Farther to the south, I went to Hantchang, Changsa, and to the village where Mao Tse-tung was born. Then I traveled to Hanchow, and to Shanghai, where I had lived for several months nine years earlier. I witnessed the activities of the first commune near Peking. Finally I returned to Peking, to be present for the celebration of the Tenth Anniversary of the People's Republic.

Reading this list of cities, one might be tempted to believe that they are no farther apart than Paris and Lyon. If so, it would be helpful to compare the distances with maps of China and France in hand.

Since my return I have often been asked these questions:

"What are the Chinese like?"

In two words, they are as old as thousands of years and as young as a few.

"Did they let you work freely?"

Yes and no. Like distances, liberty is a relative notion. It is a notion built up by one's past experiences. In short, I was authorized to photograph everything except the military. Generally, everything was made easy for me, but I still had certain difficulties in spite of my interpreter, who handled all the practical details. Perhaps, after all, these difficulties were an incentive in my work. Photography as we conceive it does not fit into the customs there, as it is considered impolite and disrespectful to take candid shots. The Chinese do not like to be photographed unawares. They respect a certain formality.

"Were you ever forbidden to take the photographs you wanted to take?"

To forbid contradicts the Chinese people's exquisite sense of politeness and reserve. When I photographed things of the past, if they happened to be somewhat run-down, my guide would draw my attention to, say, a new hospital, telling me, "It has been built since liberation."

"And what about propaganda?"

Like everybody, China wants to show her best profile; this profile is the one of the future she is building. As for the visitor, he is always free to use his eyes.

Here I have answered some of the questions that recur. The others I hope to have answered with my photographs.

January, 1972

CAPTIONS

1 A bewildered old man searches for his son as the new recruits called up by the fast-weakening Kuomintang government march off to defeat. Peking, 1949.

2 As the value of the paper money sank, the Kuomintang decided to distribute forty grams of gold per person. With the gold rush, December 1948, thousands came out and waited in line for hours. The police, equipped with the remnants of the armies of the International Concession, made only a gesture toward maintaining order. Ten people were crushed to death. Shanghai, 1948.

3 In the last days of the Kuomintang, Peking, 1949.

4 A unit of the People's Militia awaits its turn at the daily morning drill. In the background: Peking's Tien An Men Palace, where the country's leaders stand to review patriotic parades. 1957.

5 Industrial exposition: mechanical hand for handling radioactive objects. Peking, 1958.

6 Steel mill, Anshan, Manchuria, 1958.

7 A professor corrects his class papers by the lake in the newly built King Chan Park, Peking, 1958.

8 Schoolboys rest after their daily drill in the Shiu Shin Commune near Peking. Sons of peasants, they form a militia trained in the handling of guns, hand grenades, and such enemy agents as might be dropped from planes. Slogan on the wall: "Everybody loves to work." 1958.

9 An oil worker in Yumen, in the Gobi Desert, beats her drum as she leads a delegation to administration headquarters to announce their production quotas. 1958.

10 Visitors take notes on a peasant invention at National Farm Implements Exhibit, Peking, 1958.

HENRI CARTIER-BRESSON

1 *Peking, 1949*

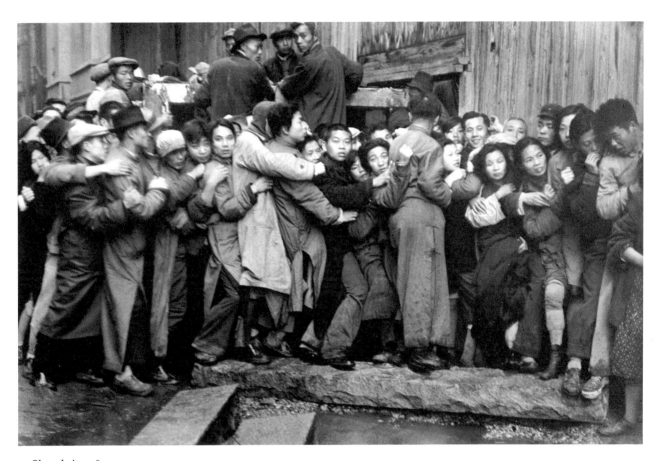

2 *Shanghai, 1948*

HENRI CARTIER-BRESSON

3 *Peking, 1949*

4 *Peking, 1957*

HENRI CARTIER-BRESSON

5 *Peking, 1958*

6 *Anshan, 1958*

HENRI CARTIER-BRESSON

7 *Peking, 1958*

8 *Near Peking, 1958*

HENRI CARTIER-BRESSON

9 *Yumen, 1958*

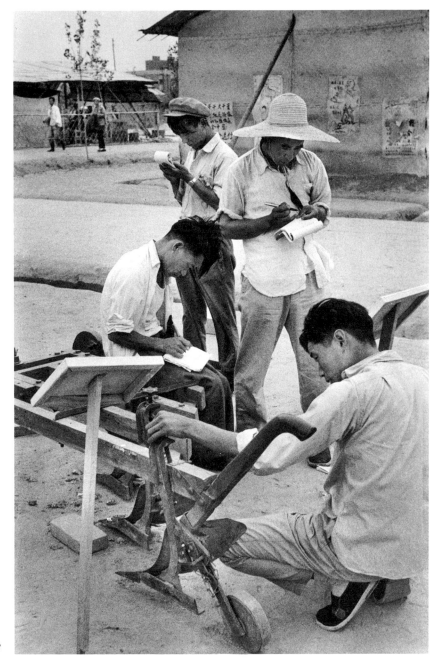

10 *Peking, 1958*

HENRI CARTIER-BRESSON

VI

MARC RIBOUD

I have spent nine months in China: four in 1957, four in 1965, one in 1971. Always, as though obsessed, I have wanted to return there to see again what I have already seen, and to see more.

It is through visual observations, more than any other means, that one can try to know and understand China today. What does the average Chinese think? A foreigner, even one fluent in the language, cannot answer since a candid communication today with a Chinese is rare. The Chinese tells you how things ought to be, rather than how they are. The "party line" is repeatedly recited by its faithful believers. That is why the best, and possibly the only way, to discover China is to look at it.

The first visual impression is that of clean austerity and poverty. In the countryside, I still saw dried-mud, thatched-roofed houses corroded by age; faded clothes patched up innumerable times; tools stained by years of wear and tear. Until not so long ago the very landscape itself was worn out; roads and paths looked more like the footprints left by millions of passers-by, rather than routes laid out by plan; and there were no more trees. But that was the image of the China of the past—a heritage of several thousands of years of history, when individual survival was the only motivation.

Now a new image, one of considerable change, is evident everywhere, fighting against the old one. Millions of trees are planted, canals are dug, roads, railroads, and factories are built. The most remote village has its school. And above all, one sees new men with a new dignity.

Indeed, what the Chinese leaders want is to build a new kind of man—one no longer motivated by the profit motive, but inspired by self-denial, a collective spirit, and the will to pursue the World Revolution. Every Chinese reads Mao Tse-tung, whose central ideas are to avoid the formation of a new class and to create a society where material recompense is absent. The battle is directed against the primacy of the city over the country, of the intellectual over the manual, of the official over the common man.

Moral rigor and discipline make today's Chinese way of life severe. The decadent excesses of the past probably explain the present-day excesses in austerity. But the austerity may also be an economic necessity. The amount of improvement yet to be accomplished is enormous. If a small group improves its standard of living, it will then become more difficult to improve the standards for the masses.

This struggle against the recrudescence of individualism is called the "struggle against modern revisionism." It was the main slogan of the Cultural Revolution. Little is yet known outside China of this revolution inside the Revolution, but it may one day prove to be the most important event in recent Chinese history, with fundamental consequences to the present and future life of every Chinese man and woman.

A Westerner may resent this way of life, but present-day China is not a country for immigrants or tourists. China is not interested in pleasing the foreigner. Her problem and her pride is to thrust into the twentieth century 800 million people born in misery. Her mission is to remain revolutionary.

January, 1972

CAPTIONS

1 On the Great Wall, Peking, 1971. As is customary, this army officer wears no insignia of rank; the camera is Chinese made.

2 On posters, everyone moves symbolically leftward. Shanghai dockyard, 1965.

3 Manpower is used to tow boats up the Yangtze. Chungking, 1957.

4 In a densely populated province, every inch of fertile land must be cultivated. Szechuan, 1957.

5 Construction of the first bridge ever to span the Yangtze River, linking North and South China. Hankow, 1957.

6 A soldier of the People's Liberation Army stands guard before the People's Palace. Peking, 1971.

7 Kang Hsi Chung, a leading dancer in "White Hair Girl," a revolutionary ballet. She wears a Mao Badge. Before her is a copy of Mao Tse-tung's *Little Red Book*. Peking, 1971.

8 A divorce court, Peking, 1965. Though recognized by the constitution, divorce is not encouraged.

9 Lui Li Chang, the street long famous for its art and antique shops. Peking, 1965.

10 Lovers in a park on a Sunday afternoon, Shanghai, 1971. Today, many girls in Shanghai have short hair instead of the traditional pigtail.

1 *Peking, 1971*

MARC RIBOUD

2 *Shanghai, 1965*

3 *Chungking, 1957*

MARC RIBOUD

4 *Szechuan, 1957*

5 *Hankow, 1957*

MARC RIBOUD

6 *Peking, 1971*

7 *Peking, 1971*

MARC RIBOUD

8 *Peking, 1965*

9 *Peking, 1965*

MARC RIBOUD

10   *Shanghai, 1971*

MARC RIBOUD

VII

RENE BURRI

I will never forget the spring evening in 1964 when, in a hotel in Olympia, I came home to find a telegram from Peking. I was in Greece to cover the story of the Olympics; the telegram invited me to Peking. China's first air link with the outside world was about to be inaugurated, and I was asked to photograph it.

Three days later I stood in Tien An Men Square in Peking and took pictures of a million Chinese men, women, and children celebrating May Day.

When I was back in Switzerland, I realized of course that I had caught but a fleeting glimpse of that vast country, then almost as mysterious to the West as in the days of Marco Polo. I decided to try everything to get back in. One year to the day I received the visa to return.

My wife and I had been given five weeks in China. But an understanding began to develop between me and my hosts, and presently my time was extended to five months, an unheard-of period for a Western journalist.

I won't pretend China can be understood in five months. But it did give me time to film not just one but several documentaries. We traveled everywhere, fifteen thousand miles in all, and were given a freedom to move we had never expected. I had been led to believe that here was a nation where people might be more like robots than human beings. It was a great discovery to me to find that this was not so. The will of the individual was subordinated to the commonweal, but people seemed to find pride and pleasure in that rather than frustration.

There were many little nuances that showed an effort to please. When we got off the train after a long journey, an interpreter would be awaiting us, and he would greet us by name. He would take us to a local irrigation station and study our faces as he tried to hide his own awe at this concrete accomplishment of the revolution: irrigation for a barren countryside.

We had the grand tour. When I wasn't filming, I was taking still photographs. Some people resented that, in the traditional Chinese manner, but others, like any girl or boy in New York or London, would start to comb their hair or straighten their clothes. And when we unexpectedly wanted to photograph a commune or a street scene our hosts would hastily straighten up the place and try and make it look as shiny as a Hollywood movie set. It took many long sessions over endless cups of tea before I could convince them to let me shoot their reality as it looked, to let me intrude into their lives.

On one of my last days in the country, I watched three Europeans walk into the dining room of my hotel. They carried spaghetti, olive oil, and Parmesan cheese. They were obviously Italian, and they showed the cook in sign language how to cook the dish for them.

Presently, the spaghetti à la Parmegiana came from the kitchen, and the Italians, very pleased, praised the Chinese talent for learning from the West. They didn't know (and I resisted the temptation to go over and tell them) that spaghetti was introduced into Italy by Marco Polo, after he had found it in China.

June, 1972

CAPTIONS
1 Lung Men caves, Loyang, 1965.
2 Kun Ming Lake, at the Summer Palace outside Peking, 1964.
3 Terraced fields for growing millet, near Yenan, 1965.
4 Monument to the Revolution, Tien An Men Square, Peking, 1964.
5 Cave of Chairman Mao Tse-tung after the Long March of 1934–35, Yenan, 1964.
6 May Day, Tien An Men Square, Peking, 1964.
7 Demonstration against American interference in the Congo, Tien An Men Square, Peking, 1964.
8 May Day, Peking, 1964.

1 *Near Loyang, 1965*

RENE BURRI

2 *Summer Palace, 1964*

3 *Near Yenan, 1965*

RENE BURRI

4 *Peking, 1964*